W9-ARQ-694

Peaceful Piggy Meditation

by Kerry Lee MacLean

Albert Whitman & Company
Chicago, Illinois

To my sweet daughter, Tessa,
Queen of Loving Kindness

Library of Congress Cataloging-in-Publication Data

MacLean, Kerry Lee.
Peaceful piggy meditation / written and illustrated by Kerry Lee MacLean.
p. cm.
Summary: Peaceful pigs demonstrate the many benefits of meditation.
[1. Meditation—Fiction. 2. Pigs—Fiction.] I. Title.
PZ7.M22436Pi 2004 [Fic]—dc22 2004000526

Published in 2004 by Albert Whitman & Company
ISBN 978-0-8075-6389-2

Printed in China
10 9 8 7 6 5 4 3 2 1 LP 20 19 18 17 16

For information about Albert Whitman & Company,
visit our web site at www.albertwhitman.com.

Sometimes the world can be such a

busy, noisy place.

Sometimes it feels like you **always** have to hurry, hurry, hurry...

and you feel like you can't **slow down**—
even when you're **sitting down!**

It can be hard **not** to lose your **temper** when you're **angry**.

And you can get **really frustrated**
when things don't go **your way.**

So it's good to have a **peaceful place inside...**

Peaceful piggies know when to take a break,

find a quiet spot, and just

breathe, breathe, breathe.

Mom or Dad might help them set up

a **special place** with a few things...

maybe a crystal, for clear thinking,

a stone, for stillness,

or even a flower, for **kindness.**

Peaceful piggies

sit like a king or queen

on their throne,

feeling the solid earth

beneath them and the

big sky all around them.

Every day, they sit

feeling their breath

going **in** and **out**

until their minds

calm down.

So peaceful piggies feel **free** like a **bird in the sky**

and as calm as a pond on a cool, clear night.

This makes it easier to **accept things** that happen and **stop wishing** for things to be **different.**

When you're **peaceful**,
you can be **truly fearless**!

Best of all, when you're feeling peaceful, you like who you are, just as you are.

So it's easier to face

the truth about yourself...

and it's easier to stand **up**
to **others**.

Happy Birthday!

Peaceful piggies take **good care** of their friends...

and their **enemies** too.

They try to be **loving** and **kind** to **all beings...**

even **worms.**

By **slowing down**, peaceful piggies notice all the magical little things in life—like the way raindrops race one another down the window...

the way the **clouds** tell **silent** stories...

and the way birds sing songs **just for you.**

Having a peaceful place inside
helps keep a happy heart happy,
so that even on a horrible...

painful...

disgustingly
rotten day...

a **peaceful piggy** can

smile.

Peaceful Piggy Meditation

Find a quiet place to sit on the floor. Use a pillow to sit on.

Sit like the piggies: cross-legged, with a straight back, looking down at the ground about two feet in front of you.

Ring a gong or a bell to start. (If you don't have either, a metal mixing bowl makes a nice sound when you strike it with a pencil.)

As you breathe in, feel the cool air through your nose, then feel the warmer air that you breathe out. Try counting each breath.

Feel your thoughts and emotions settling down as you sit still. If you feel your thoughts creeping in again, slow down. Let your thoughts go, and just be aware of your breaths going in and out, in and out.

Try doing this for five minutes. It may seem hard at first, but do it as long as you can—long enough to feel peaceful.

Ring the gong or bell to end. Don't move yet. Wait until you can't hear the gong anymore. Enjoy the moment.

Remember this quiet feeling. Imagine that you keep it deep inside yourself all day long.

Keep this rule of thumb in mind: One hour of meditation for adults = one minute for children. (Our brains are that different!)

☆ Mind-in-a-Jar Experiment ☆

You'll need:

- Large glass jar
- Long-handled spoon for stirring
- A handful of glitter, foil confetti, or potting soil

Fill the jar with clean water. Imagine the jar is your mind.

Then drop the glitter, confetti, or soil into the water. These are your thoughts and feelings.

If you want, you can add the materials in small handfuls instead of all at once. Let each handful stand for a particular thought or emotion, saying each one out loud.

Or, if you have different-colored glitter or confetti, you can name a color for each emotion, such as red for angry thoughts, blue for sad thoughts, and green for excited thoughts.

Use the spoon to stir up the water and the materials, making them swirl around like a tornado. Or put a lid on the jar and shake it.

This is what your mind is like when you're stressed out or late for school or fighting with friends or family.

Think about how you feel when your mind is like this. Are you confused? Stressed? Scared? Overwhelmed?

Stop stirring and remove the spoon. Or, if you're shaking the jar, set it down. Now watch the particles slowly drift down to the bottom as the water—and your mind—becomes calm and clear. Notice how peaceful you feel as the water clears itself of all the thoughts.

You can use the mind jar exercise as part of your meditation ritual. Try sitting in your mediation position with the jar in front of you, then ring the gong after you've stirred or shaken the jar. Ring the gong once more when the water in the jar has settled and become clear.

Teachers can keep a mind jar in the classroom for students to use when they need it.

About Family Meditation

Can you imagine an entire family getting up early just to practice peacefully being together for a few minutes? Now imagine what it would be like for a child to carry that experience with him for the rest of the day. Meditation is a lifelong discipline that, when practiced daily, soothes the mind and calms the emotions, giving both children and adults an invaluable still point within.

My husband and I raised five children while following hectic schedules. When we began making time to meditate with our kids every day, we noticed our children were nicer, happier, and more peaceful and confident. Sometimes our kids loved the quiet time together and other times they resisted it, but they began to understand it as a self-care regimen. "You brush your teeth to keep your mouth clean; you meditate to keep your mind clean," we explained. They accepted this and as adults they willingly brush their teeth and love meditating on their own.

It may be hard to believe that pausing to meditate together just a few minutes a day could make such a difference, but give it a try for three months and see for yourself. I saw it in my own family and I see it all the time in the families I work with.

Kerry Lee MacLean
Certified Children's Meditation Instructor
Shambhala Children's Rites of Passage Elder